NAVIGATING
THE QUARTZ FOREST

NAVIGATING
THE QUARTZ FOREST

B I M A N   R O Y

ARPress
ILLUMINATING IDEAS
EMPOWERING VOICES

Designed by Author Reputation Press, LLC.
Cover art by Biman Roy
Author photo by Glenn Losack, MD

ARPress
45 Dan Road Suite 5
Canton MA 02021

Hotline: 1(800) 220-7660
Fax: 1(855) 752-6001

Ordering Information:
Quantity sales. Special discounts are available on quantity purchases by corporations, associations, and others. For details, contact the publisher at the address above.

Printed in the United States of America.

ISBN-13:	Paperback	979-8-89330-783-2
	eBook	979-8-89330-784-9
	Hardback	979-8-89330-785-6

Library of Congress Control Number: 2024904016

To Sumona Roy, whose notes served as the primary inspiration for these poems.

Contents

Officially BF

~~[illegible strikethrough]~~

~~[illegible strikethrough]~~

~~[illegible]~~

127 hours

~~[illegible strikethrough]~~

1

On Measurement

There is always an urge to measure.
How many, how long, how heavy?
Metric or nonmetric,
To assuage and conform—

Even the heart's rendition
Of a wailing horn
In night's church.

You say, 'miles to go',
I say, 'light as a feather',
You say, 'high as a kite'
I say, 'deep shit'.

You don't deal with
Oblong issues,
I don't weep mountain roses,
Just to break the back
Of the universe
And be in command.

You say, "Officially BF
Dot dot dot—
127 hours"

I say, "Look out
Through the window,
The bed of impatiens
In the westerly sun."

She got slapped for talking

Finale was intense
Burning houses

Sometimes I'm in character. It
doesn't matter. Nothing Matters.

In Character

It arrives like an urge to itch
At an awkward moment
But you are forced to sit still
And go through the visuals.

Must be in a black & white
WWII movie, I am not sure
What was I doing when I saw it?
Was it in a theater or on the TV?

Darkness at noon, a girl 8 or 9,
The room was cold and numb
To the world, entered mother,
The girl was talking when shots
Fired outside and steps neared.

Mother to the window,
The girl kept talking,
Mother panicked and
Slapped her for talking
And dragged her into the cellar.

Finale was intense and
The scene closes on burning houses.

Sometimes I am in character.
It does not matter then.

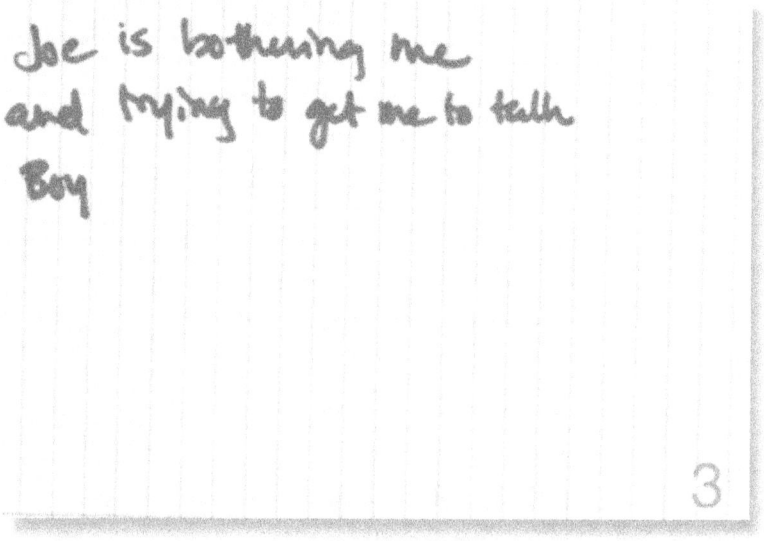

Joe is bothering me
and trying to get me to talk

Boy

3

Some Mornings

Some mornings are chatty.
All kinds of birds,
Murmuring of leaves,
Even the fishes in the glass prison
Nibble on algae loudly
And a mother talking to her daughter
While waiting for the school bus.

Then there are mornings
That hang like a wrung shirt
From clothespins,
Wet and silent, under a gray sky.

Not much commerce between girls
In the neighborhood and
Phone is off the hook,
Inside of you the shutters are down,

Everything seems to bother,
Even joy.

Congrats on the
wedding! I can't
tall
That's fair

wine   4

Destination Wedding

As night falls
The band swings into action.
Fireworks lit the interior
Of ribcages,
Coyotes of doubt run deep,
As a hammer hitting on the nail.

Then the full picture
Emerges slowly in piecemeal.
First from the southwest
Corner of the frame
Then the northeast,
From emptiness onward.

You say, "Congrats on the wedding."
She says, "I can't talk."
You say, "That's fair wine."

Once the fox retreats
The snowy glimmer of rabbits
Inhabit the land.

Greg said I can't ~~tell ya~~
Our friendship depends on it
What's Kevin's costume?
It's fun!
Band of Brothers   5

Life on Earth

Some relationships seem to be impervious
Like proverbial appliances—
Rust proof, waterproof, scratch proof,
Even child proof and the machine
Keeps its chatter unabated.

You say, "I can't talk."
"But how can I?
Our friendship depends on it."

Angry words, loving words,
Both needed to tighten the knot
As light pours into night.

When curse, kiss, sneer and smile
Frolic around lips
As a band of brothers,
Then it's a fun as a Halloween costume.

How are you?   Are you
NOLA   caught up on
Pharmacy Museum   Scandal?

Fat cat?

You have to get through the
1st couple of eps though

6

Looking for an Answer

Sometimes you ask questions
Those are morning mist like,
Nebulous, evanescent.
Not meaning to seek an answer,
So that the echo comes
Back to you uncoupled.

When you asked, "How are you, Nola?"
You actually meant,
"Are you caught up on Scandal?"
So, any answer will sound
As a shadow answer or no answer.

When we say words that are not
Solid as feldspar, it scatters like
Refracted beams of light.

So, when you ask, "Where is Fat Cat?"
She says, "In the pharmacy museum."

Once you go through a couple
Of crystal episodes you learn
How easily the needle moves
In and out of the moleskin
And the air through the clothesline.

I wanted to
do a tour,
but we didn't
have time
too many people

7

Obstacles

Between wanting to do something
And doing it,
There is an invisible pause
Like a comma or a semicolon.

Weighing in sometimes
An inclement weather,
A nasty headache, even childbirth,
Or more terrible news like
The river washing away
The fate line off your hand.

You work hard
As a nest building bird
Or a winter rat, to take
A trip to the mountain.
Then face a *No Entry* sign
By a Mining magnet
Or just before riding
To a ski slope your pelvis caves in.

You say to your neighbor,
"I wanted to do a tour,
But we didn't have time
And too many people."

Aaccyea

What!?

Their
Fantasy
League

Hot chocolate

I like it though

8

Getting it Right

Don't ask the poet.
Ask the poem, instead
If you fail to get IT.

He is just a conduit.
Don't embarrass him.

Why ask the flute
That let the breath pass
To the other end
To morph into music?

Even then—
Suppose you don't,
So what?

You don't ask
Hot chocolate!!
You say, "I like it though".

Now you are a part
Of a fantasy league
Navigating your own galaxy.

I'm so mad Logan is
during Parker. That is so stupid

Tim though?!.!? He killed
the Dean!

I just saw the op where lowe
says he wants to run
Ed Begly Junior for sherriff

9

Impressions

Moving on a cart in slow motion
You put stickers on faces, manners,
Incidents, accidents as you pass.

Some fall off, some remain,
Like dream fragments
Or competing memory of
An awkward uncle in a family wedding
Or as a side talk—
"I am so mad Logan is dating Parker.
That's so stupid"

They mill around like confused pilgrims
In a wild terrain.
You live their bewilderment
As you pass through so many gates
Empty handed or pleasure treasured.

You don't care if someone hiked the dream
Or someone wants to run for Sheriff.

Then a time comes like moments before
A ripe fruit leaps on to ground,
You say, "I am through!!"
While still in the passage.

what's the app?

Spaceteam

He's mad

I'm getting sleepy

I'm thinking I am

10

Looking for Self in a Quartz Forest

Last night we were in a quartz forest
Where trees beamed themselves on to others
Instantly, as you fixed your eyes on one.

Was it a myrtle, juniper or jacaranda?
Hard to tell, or any tree for that matter.

Frustrated I asked, "what app?
Trickster or Space Team?"

You were counting something
With your fingers—
Photons, decibels or gigabytes.

"He is mad," I was saying to myself
But looking for an excuse
I said, "I am getting sleepy."

You looked at me as you have
For thousands of years and said,
"I am thinking I am"

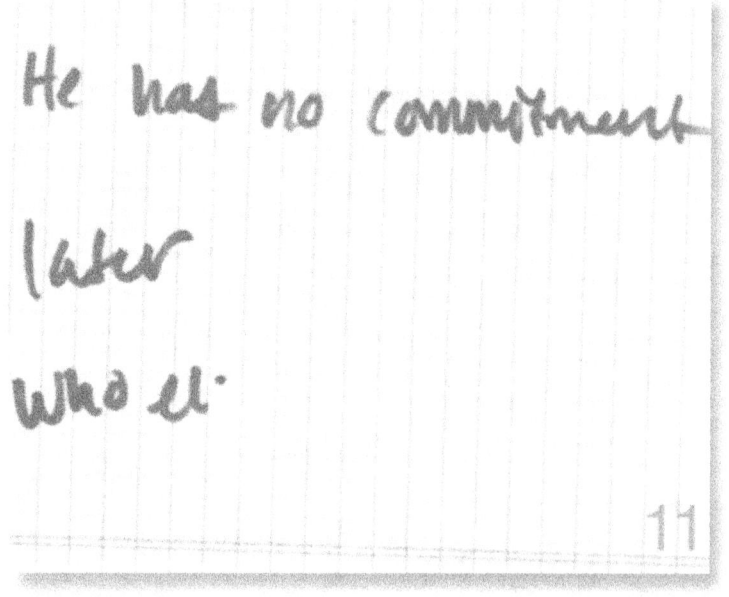

He has no commitment

later

who el·

11

Expectation, Commitment

When two brothers or a couple
Walk side by side or hand in hand,
Walking with the shadow—
Expectation, Commitment.

The day opens with music.
The tendril moves toward sun,
The postman sharp at noon,
Rush hour train right on time.
Expectation, commitment.

When it fails to happen
You say, "He has no commitment."

Then as in a little wild sister
Or a jealous dog
Randomness pushes
Into the space between.

Later, resigned you say,
"What else can one do?"
You can't be angry at the weatherman!

What did we do last sat?

There were cats and t
was ALLERGIX!

I was Gamora

12

Buckled Pines, Hurt Moon

Memory can't hold the rain.
The old canopy
And the weight of wetness.

"What did we do
Last Saturday?"

"There were cats
And I was ALLERGIX."

You looked through
Buckled pines.
A hurt moon looked back.

We were Gomorrah.

Now the fever is gone,
So also fear.

Still, a stilled restlessness
Before the execution.

Besides Binder, I get to talk to
people I like on thursday anyways
Girls

Girls night
But I love you
The most!
So I would want to talk to you

13

Because I Love You

Sundays were always church
In my young Catholic years,
Then football took over.

Girls' night on Saturdays,
Wednesdays, gym and music lesson,
I like to talk to people on Thursdays.

Things tow the same line—
Snow boots in winter, shorts in summer.

Needs shift while changing jobs,
Taking new lovers, the seat
Next to you stays vacant sometimes,
Eager looks sweep past the crowd.

Hard to convince someone then
That you would like to talk to him only
Because you love him the most.

We're going to go
I'm sorry

14

Parting

Always the same story—
Tea in old China, a little pastry
Bought from the corner bakery
Mixed with gossips and giggles,

Talks, mostly meaningless
To a listening stranger,
Like two neighbors on a stoop,
In a foreign language.

Then a sudden rush—
Heart jumps into the mouth,
"Are you leaving?"
"We are going to go,"
A little pause, "I am sorry."

A below the radar quiver
Passes over the face, weightless,
A desire to hold slowly retreats—
A deer into the woods.

Mike, You look great !

~~Breakfast~~ Turtle

I love this and I'm sorry
You have to keep holding
my ~~win~~

15

Playacting

You look great in your jade turtleneck.
As you surf past through the sea of people,
I bloom into a flower of stone.

I hold you in my eyes, filling up as a green pond
As I hang like a pendant from a silver thread,
Unobtrusive.

All through the evening we keep talking nonessentials,
Tiptoeing around secret tulips.
Playacting makes me feel safe from myself.

Two hours into the party you are all smiles.
I said, "I love this, but I am sorry
You have to keep holding my wine."

NOTHING MATTERS

Are you feeling good?

For the 10 minutes

Carrie

woodcliff manor
warehouse
Dist.

zoo!

Magazine
St!

sorry

Are you feeling drunk

Don't be mad at me

sorry

16

Nothing Matters

The way a squirrel fondles
The dried apricot
Or the osprey swoops down
To the heart of the marsh
With its hungry beak,
The haunted manor—

Wet hands in sweat
Feel the heft of flesh
Arranged on racks,
Even the music, dead in track
Fails to surprise.

Beyond the cliff
Its warehouse filled with bones
Torches the night.

The magazine street
Ends in the zoo district
Where you can feel
The silk of silt
On ducks' backs.

Are you feeling dark?
Or are you saying sorry, sorry
Just to oblige?

O life, don't get mad at me—
Matters that nothing there is.

on ep. 17 of Season 3   17

I love your costume!
Abigail Adams
G1 Jane   what happened?
Eric?
Thank you so much!
          I can't wait!   17

Even When You Are Gone

Two maples in the back yard,
Adam and Abigail,
In gold blond and red radiance
On the morning of Halloween.

You walk up to them and say,
"I love your costumes"
And pat on their trunks.

Years before they survived
Sandy's fury with the help of
G.I. Jane, they were younger then.

Evil blight, deadly bugs,
Ruckus of the wind and
As the drapery falls off
They stand naked in the cold.

You feel a tender ache,
How long can you protect them?
Worries run wild
Like quick-footed squirrels—

As a proud mother you watch,
Their tips have topped the roof
And you say, "I can't wait
Until the next batch of splendor
Comes to surprise me."

www.ingramcontent.com/pod-product-compliance
Lightning Source LLC
Chambersburg PA
CBHW060357130626
46553CB00003B/1274